Being True To One's Self

Being True To One's Self

By: Sabrina Gregory

iUniverse, Inc.
New York   Bloomington

Being True To One's Self

This is a work of fiction. All of the characters, names, incidents, organizations, and dialogue in this novel are either the products of the author's imagination or are used fictitiously.

iUniverse books may be ordered through booksellers or by contacting:

iUniverse
1663 Liberty Drive
Bloomington, IN 47403
www.iuniverse.com
1-800-Authors (1-800-288-4677)

ISBN: 978-1-4401-2977-3 (pbk)
ISBN: 978-1-4401-2978-0 (ebk)

Printed in the United States of America

iUniverse rev. date: 5/5/2009

This book of poems represents my life and the people that have crossed my path. Life is an experience and the book is my walk through the woods called life.

So enjoy the adventure and tell me what you think. Thank you in advance for taking the time to read me.

Thank you
Sabrina Gregory
Sabrina Gregory

Alonzo

Your name means fight and a fighter you are.
Against many odds and obstacles you came into our lives.
So strong you are my little one.
So determined to get what you desire.
Your presence in a room lights up like a bright star.
Your smile brightens everyone.
Uniting a divided family that's what you did.
Patching up a hole in my heart- giving my life new meaning.
My sweet child the joy you bring. I only hope that our
family gives you the same.

An Encounter

A chance encounter that's what it was. A once in a lifetime opportunity. Who knew that we would meet again? What were the odds of us meeting once more? That concerned look, those soft eyes and that beautiful smile.

I looked up and there you were. A familiar face across the crowd. What I found is one in a trillion. We are so much alike in so many ways. So many things have fallen into place. Can this friendship be true?

Only one way to find out. Open Pandora's Box and we will find a gem. A jewel, a great surprise my man.

ANTHONY-MAN CHILD

Anthony man with those big brown eyes. Eyes that are reflective of myself. Anthony has the heart of a lion and the strength of an elephant. He's strong willed and determined to make a mark in the world. Never underestimate Anthony nothing will get in his way to success.

Anthony has many sides to his hyperactive self. He's so full of life. Life is a ball game to him. A soft side to man that no one else sees. He is loving and caring. He will protect his own. Like a lion protecting his cubs. I love my son because he's the man. No matter what he will always be my rock and my reason for living.

Baby Momma Drama

Feeling trapped and out of the loop. Trying to be the mature one. Getting small pieces of info when it's only necessary. Over hearing conversations and feeling left out. It's like a quarter back playing and not knowing the game plan.

Making decisions being made without me being consulted. Feeling that I'm being left out in the cold. Trying to hold on to what's not really yours. Sharing time being pushed into a corner. It's not easy being the other woman in this little game. Baby momma drama is not easy to play. Seeing the light at the end of the tunnel. Being patient it will all come?

At the end she's only holding on to what was once her's. Knowing that I'm the only woman he wants to come home to. I know that other women have felt the same way. Feeling that the past is affecting your present. It's like a little kid; they only want a toy when someone else is playing with it. If it wasn't for the kids I don't think I could bear it.

The women playing chess, no one will see that plan till the queen is taken at the last minute. I guess she thinks I will give up and run. I have a good man and you could not see that. So back up, and get you a new man. Being the bigger person is so hard. Taking the high road is never easy. I guess I will have to make a way to deal with this whole thing. But I will not take my eye off you. A rat in the garden will be eaten by the snake.

Betrayal

Betrayal- dishonesty- lies and untruths are the worst word in the dictionary. Trust is gone, faith is nonexistent. The only thing you can do is stay on your toes and hope that the next line will be true. True to your heart and to oneself. Taking a leap of faith can be hard. One must take a chance and fly. It is so easy to hate and take revenge. It's so easy to scream and raise your hands.

I've stared at a screaming man. A scarred man looking at the sea of lies in someone's eyes. I will not give into your lies.

I will not die or give up my fight, I WILL **STAY STRONG AND LIVE TO FIGHT ANOTHER FIGHT.**

<u>Bitch</u>

You know when a woman is bad she gets what ever she wants. When a woman is a bitch no one stands in her way. When a woman gets mean all hands are on deck. But when a woman is nice, she get no respect. When a women is pleasant she gets no props.

When there is no drama, no fire, no fight- she gets no love, no time and no attention. I guess I should go back to being a **BITCH** because at least I would be heard. I should yell and scream. I would be noticed. When you're a bitch you won't be bitten in the ass. Walk in someone else's shit.

I should be a bitch so I can bite people in the ass. I should be a bitch so that I could be first at the line. I guess it pays to be a bitch, because a bitch will never be last. Holding on to so much anger can't be fun. Making the world pay for what should be mine. A good dog will get her way. Living with no fears or regrets. Maybe the flip side is cool. Everyone loves a bad girl, a rough neck, a battle ready to happen

<u>BLIND</u>

I WAS BLIND TO THINK I COULD CHANGE HIS MIND. I WAS FOOLISH TO THINK I WAS WORTHY OF HIS LOVE AGAIN AND BE HAPPY.

I THOUGHT HE WOULD FINALY CHOOSE ME.

BUT I WAS CONFIDENT ENOUGH TO GIVE HIM A CHOICE. A SMALL LIGHT AT THE END THE TUNNEL. A LITTLE CON DOESN'T HURT IF IT HELPS YOUR TEAM.

LOVE IS BLIND, BUT PEOPLE CAN SEE. THEY SEE WHAT THEY WANT TO SEE. IT MAY NOT BE PRETTY OR SEXY. LOVE HAS NO RULES OR LIMITS. NO ONE CAN CHANGE OR BEND IT. TRUE LOVE IS EVEN WORSE, BECAUSE IT HOLDS ON TO YOUR HEART.

BLIND AS A BAT I WILL BE. IT IS BETTER TO HAVE LOST, THAN NOT LOVED AT ALL.

Brown Eyes- Marcus

Since you were six I watched you grow into a young smart gentleman. The apple of my eye. I only hope the world treats you fair. Wish I could be the fly on the wall when you meet the right girl. She will see the greatness in you and how special you are.

Anyone who gets you will be lucky to have you. A knight in shining armor. Hold the door, say please and thank you and may I help you. You will be great when it's time. Enjoy life on your terms. Don't fall in life's traps. Life will throw you a bone. Stay on the right track. Be true to the game. Brown eyes, through my eyes I can see that you are very special.

Your parents have given you a great start. Teaching you to follow your own heart. Take the road less traveled and be an adventurer. No one likes a follower because they have no brains. Marcus you're my other son and I love being in your life. Your smile and good humor. Your voice a bear's, you run like a cheetah and no one can compare to you.

I guess you have impressed me so much I do not see any flaws. Life is hard and tough. Love is better. Letting you live a life with no bonders or rules to follow. Make good choices and be your own person. Grow up like your father, who is a great father and provider. I know your mother is very proud of you. But I'm your cheerleader on the side lines. Can I be there when you become a great leader, standing in front of millions. Make a difference and help all in your path.

Marcus you stand tall and think big. Take advantage of good fortune. Don't ever turn your back on the little man. That same man may pull you out of a ditch. The quicksand of life can drown you. Be strong, walk tall and think outside the box. Marcus I'm so proud of you, the great person that you are. Love always till the end of time, your cheerleader on the side lines.

CHILDREN

From a small egg and sperm an embryo is created. Love nurtured from birth. Babies are one's beautiful creations. Their unconditional love so pure. There is no other love of a child, no greater gift than anyone can give you. Children need love and attention. No pain or harm. I knew children can change one's life. Turn it inside out, up and down all around. Children may drive me mad. But on the other hand our lives would not be complete without them. My children give me hope. Little bundles that God has given me. I've had great experiences through their eyes. No matter what I want them to succeed to grow and improve this world.

Children will blossom and make a difference. They will bring hope and happiness to this planet. Sometimes yes they may be brats, but they're all mine. They did not ask to be brought into this world.

Children are our present and future. Children are our great leaders and rulers

of the universe. Futures
that are so bright. The future is a pearl
in the oyster. They are bright light and
shinning stars.

<u>Choice</u>

Life has many choices and during ones life we must make decisions. Whether to go left or right. To go straight or back up.

The only choice in life that hurts is the choice to love or not to love. Life is too short not to take chances. But being hurt or crushed is the worst pain of all.

The next choice is to choose to stay in love or move on. What if the choice was not given to you but another. The only choice you are left is to feel the love till the love is gone. To hold and hope. Hope that the other person is kind and can make the transition as smooth as possible.

My choice right now is to love a man, who I've called my soul mate. Cut the love now and begin the healing process. Falling in love is fun and easy.

But falling out of love is not easy. Loving yourself and thinking it's okay to love again.

The choice is cut and dried. If you apply too much pressure, you will lose. If you do not, you may lose him anyway. But you're a fighter and you continue to choose to go down fist waving in the air. Fighting for that love and happiness.

Day of Rest

Day of rest who said you rest. Playing catch up is the name of the game. Do the laundry, clean house, make three square meals and by the way have a life.

There doesn't seem to be enough time in the day to get rest. Make things fit in a small time frame. But one thing I try to do is smell the roses, appreciate what I have and enjoy my family. Get set go, race to the finish line called life.

<u>Emotions</u>

Trying to hold back the tears, that are falling. Trying to stop my heart from hurting. My heart beats so hard and so fast. My chest can't keep my heart from breaking thru.

The feeling came hard and fast. The ride of emotions so fast. Emotions are a bitch to control. Emotions can take a hold on you. Reaching in the bag and pulling out the right one.

The right time, the right place and the right feeling get stuck. Being a woman is complex. The stars are not aligned, the sea has parted and the ground shakes. The emotions are a hard ride to take. Being a woman is hard a road to travel. Emotions define me. The moods are up and down.

Emotions feeling sane one minute and totally losing my mind. Girls can you feeling them going round and round. Hot, cold, calm before the storm. My emotions are going, going, gone. Madness feels so close I can see it's beating eyes. I can taste it, feeling the other side. Take control one day at a time.

Emotions will not get the best of me. Like the rodeo I will lasso you up and tie it down. My emotions will not get the best of me.

FAMILY

A family doesn't consist of a mother, father and son.

A family may be many other things or people.

My family is vast and mighty, large or small

My family has unconditional love, not connected to money or blood.

My family keeps me strong and at this time; my family gives me strength.

A strength that can not be measured in ounces or pounds.

The strength of this family gives me hope, spirit and the will to continue.

Family that will be by your side.

Feeling Scared

I'm getting scared, hell yea!!!!
I'm feeling insecure. The feeling of the
unknown consumes me.

Why be a chicken? Just do it, go a head.
That leap of faith. Jump into the water- just go.
Face first!!!

Just go on and live. Try not to go back go
forward. Trying to be a warrior not a coward.

Feeling scared sucks but not feeling is not
living life AT ALL.

Finish Line

As I lay here I wonder were I'm going. I'm always running, running and running. The endless race with no Finish Line. When does the finish line come for me? Here is a pot of Gold !!!!

I wonder, I guess I need to grow up and decide what I want out of life. The hardest work is yet to come.

I'm a good woman not asking for much. Maybe I should start; demand peace, love and happiness. I think I will take the last piece of the pie. Be true to myself. Take the gold, the platinum, the silver and finish the race first.

Freedom

You give me freedom the gift no one has given
me before.
The gift of hope, when all other doors where
closed.
Through your eyes I can see light at the end of
the tunnel.

I can see the field of flowers without trees. A
free flowing river that never end. A beginning
to such happiness that's what my soul
requires.

Freedom with no boundaries, no stop signs,
and no gates. Just freedom.

Harp

I found a harp floating in the sea. Abandoned, neglected and thrown away. I picked up the harp and I knew the beautiful songs it once sang. So I dusted it off and took it home.

A diamond in the rough that no one has seen. The lovely curves, the fine wires, the notes that needed to be tuned.

It just needed some love and attention. Someone to hear its song. My harp and me are happy because we understand each other. We will never be apart.

Home

The Place where we live is small and tight.

The places where we live is all we have.

The outside world cannot break in.

The outside world cannot make us happy.

For our place is our fortress, our
Kingdom, our home.

I Know

I know it hurts.
I know you need to heal.
Time will tell.
Be strong, look within yourself.
Find the strength and courage.
You're stronger than you think.
The spirit within must surface and control the rest.
Your heart is beating loud and your brain can't
feel the pain.
We must remember all the pain he caused. All the
hateful things he said.
Remember the tears that fell from your eyes. The
pain that ran through your body.
I know that thru pain we grow and learn.
I know I must continue on and let God carry me
thru this valley.
To get to the light.

JAIME

As the car pulls up to the house and I saw this beautiful man standing there. I could not move or speak.

Time stood still. I gazed into his eyes; everything that I ever knew was about to change. When we are together time has no space or meaning. When we first kissed my heart knew from that moment on that you were the one. The one to love me, the one to hold me and I would share the rest of my life with him.

When we made love and our souls touched. I wanted to cry out "Thank You – Thank You". I could only hope that I have touched your heart, body and soul the way you have touched mine. For years you have been in my life and I saw you as a very close friend. You have stayed by my side from our teen years 'til adulthood. Your caring ears have listened to all my troubles and sadness. You were always there. You were there when I Graduated from High School; You were there when I got married. Funny thing you were ALWAYS there right under my nose.

I guess we were always there for each other. When time seemed rough or happy we were there for each other. Till it was time for us to be there for each other for life.

Jessica

Joyous
Energetic
Selfish at times
Self-confident
Incurable
Caring
Attitude

Jessica is what I'm not. Confident, cocky and sassy. She has the making of a strong independent little lady, that will never be taken advantage of.

She's courageous without a doubt . She knows what she wants out of life. Jessica is young and dangerous. Beautiful and bold describes her well. Brat, yes still my best friend and a mama's little girl.

Kids

Kind
Irreplaceable
Demanding
Silly

Kindness that they show. **Irreplaceable**- you would not trade them in for anything else. **Demanding** so much of your time and energy. **Silly** is the way they make you feel.

Kids keep you young and they break you down. Stress you out, that's what they do. But kids can give you joy. Heartache and pain all at the same time. But without kids life has no meaning, no joy and no laughter. Kids are the future and the beginning. Kids will be there til the end.

<u>LAUGHTER</u>

I miss the song of joy in her heart.
I miss the smile you gave me.
I miss the laughter .
The innocence in your heart.

Caught in the middle of the fight.
I'm sorry you could not see, what lay
beneath. What displeased me.

My only regrets. Was not being able to
hold you. Tell you, I truly loved you.

Linda

The mother to all children. The
keeper to all lost souls. You have brought
so much joy to so many children. Each
child receives unconditional love from
a person – they give unconditional love
back.

I only wish that I could be half the
woman you are. No jealousy, just love
my sister. You treat my children like they
were your own.

Mother Theresa has nothing on you
girl. Just live the life you always lead.
Pure, hopeful and full of joy.

Linda Sue

Linda Sue had so many kids what to do. Cleaning and washing a hurricane just went through. Running noses so many BOO-BOO'S changing diapers and making lunch too.

Miss Linda just had no time. What's a caretaker to do? It's naptime and playtime then it's over. Six O clock the kids are picked up.

Now she can rest with her mind free and clear. Tears and smiles have no fear. Kids are fun when they can go home.
Games and fun now her day is done.

LO-ASS

When will you grow up and be a man? When will you make a stand? Your children's lives are passing you by. Anthony will be six and Jessica too will be a woman soon.

I don't understand why you choose to close your eyes and not be a man.

Be a man and stand up for your children. Be in their lives, Call them when you can. You choose to run to another state. You choose your wife, her kids, her lifestyle and her part of the Ohio state.

Every time I think you make good on your promises to be a good father- you prove me wrong again. You're good one month then you're bad another.

You play daddy when it's convenient for you. Graduation, confirmation and report card day. Christmas and birthday's is when you try to save the day, But the summer is just a couple of months away. The whole year leading up for two short months and damn you mess that up with your stupid excuse. Excuse of being a dad and watch your kids. Excuse of staying in their life making them special in your busy life.

The kids are growing up so fast and you're not here to see it. Just another another man, **MY BABIES DADDY.**

Looking Back

How could you lie to me over and over again? Building my hopes up only to knock them down. I trusted you with all my heart. I did not lie to you. But how could you cheat me out of what I wanted. When you knew you could not give it to me without a doubt.

Life is funny and I tried to understand it. If you can't trust the one you love then who can you trust. I only hope that I can move on. To capture the innocence and lock it down. To accept the hate. When I look back it's just an experience that I will never forget. To get over and move on is chapter I in my life.

Man and Woman In Their Search For Love

When God created man from his body he created woman as his companion and his partner. But during her search for a man she found some difficulty in finding her true love or soul mate, too many demons in disguise.

Her search was like daily shopping- "taking eggs from the shelf throwing out the rotten ones." But a mere walk by the sea- mystery and treasure to explore. Finally a rare oyster- opening her oyster to find a rare pearl pure and true love.

Thus two kinds of love that will grow and blossom into the most beautiful flower. True soul mate, one mind, one soul till eternity.

Merry Go Round

Round and round making no
progress. Up and down making no
headway. Trying to go somewhere
but stuck in one spot. See
something that's not there.

Round and round we go feeling
that we can go but so far.
Talking till theres no breath
coming out. Listening with no
ears.

Where does it all end? When does
he hear me? Round and round I go
getting dizzy can't stop. Merry
goes around. Merry goes round
when will it ever stop!!!!!

MOMMA (DEE)

I LOVE MY MOM. THRU YOUR
EYES I SEE SO MUCH PAIN AND
SORROW.

YOUR LIFE I WISH I COULD
BRING YOU PEACE AND PUT IT
IN HER LAP.

GIVE BACK THE JOY, THE
SMILE. THE HOPE YOU ONCE
KNEW. I DON'T BRING HER
ANY MORE SADNESS. I JUST
WANT HER TO BE HAPPY.

MOMMA DEE I WISH I COULD
GIVE YOU THE WORLD. BRING
BACK THE SMILE TO THE MOM
I ONCE KNEW.

YOU ARE MY BEST FRIEND,
MY HEART AND THE LOVE OF
MY LIFE....

My Poems Are A Part Of Me

My poems are a part of me.
My poems have set me free.
My poems have life and meaning.
My poems are a documentary of my life, love
and grief.
So take open, each page is a piece of my flesh.
Each page is the hair of my scalp. The ink,
my blood.
Put all of the pages and chapters together and
there I am.
Open me like a book and enjoy.

My Other Half (Jessica)

You complete me. You break me down and I still stay. You drive me crazy, but I can't walk away. Child of mine you are truly mine. You're like me without a doubt. You push my buttons. You drive me to the edge. I catch myself before I fall.

I will always be there no matter what my child. Don't you worry. Don't have any doubts. A mother's love you can count on. Without you I'm not complete. My true half, my daughter, my heart and my reason for living.

My Sister (Linda)

Even though we are not blood related.
I feel that in another life we were
sisters.

My sister Linda has the patience of a
saint!!!! She's an angel on earth.
You have a kind smile, laugh and a
pure soul.

She's my idol. She makes me proud in so
many ways. I can only hope to be half
the woman you are today. Always there
when I need you most. Never judging
and a real true friend. All that you
touch turns to gold. My wish for you
my sister is to have happiness and joy.
That's what you have given me.

My Son

Such a gentle soul who carries the weight of the world on him shoulders. Such a kind heart- that I wish could not be broken. Those big eyes that weeps with you as he sees all of your pain. That sweet face that cries when life has you down. My son can be such an angel, sitting by my side. He keeps the bad guys away. To watch over me, protect me from harm. You are a gentle soul. Being my bodyguard, angel, my protector, my knight in shining armor. I only hope I have given you love as much as you have given me. My son THE MAN sweet dreams always.

MYSELF

My child has made me whole.
My husband has filled my heart with joy.
My parents have given me love and support.
I give myself time.
Time to find myself.
Time to enjoy.

Right now this moment in time has made me
happy and complete.

Right now at this moment has made me say
that I can finally be at peace.

NEW BEGININGS

Control and disarray. The beginning is so close but so far.
Trying to stay in control. When the world around you is
chaos. As I look into the sea of disarray and say help.

HELP ME......

There is always drama before the peace. Thunder before
the storm.
So hard and complicated.
You fought to come into this world and you fight to stay
alive.
What I want and what I receive is different.
I will fight to get a new life and new beginning.

Nigger

What's up nigger? The homey said to his friend. Hey nigger! The white man said. The difference between black and white is like night from day. But what's funny, they don't want to be us, but they want to look like us. They pump up their lips, they tan their skin and that drives me crazy. They try to pump up their skinny little asses. They don't want to be truly black. To walk in our skin, to carry that burden. Being black is not a trend, it's life. Being black and male is a time bomb ready to go off.

One out of four black males will go to jail. Three out of four white will go to college. The tit for tat is like Ying and Yang. One cannot exist without the other. With all of the so call blinders on- whites wanting to be black. They listen to rap; they try to walk the walk. But no matter what, young or old, educated or scholarly we will never evolve we will always be a **FUCKING NIGGER.**

No Baggage

The weight is off my shoulders. The sun shines again.
Like a knight in shining armor you have rescued me.
I can see the light at the end of the tunnel.

Lighter than a feather free as a bird. My heart is
open to you. I can feel your love, and so happiness
anchor- I can be your partner.

So glad you're my man, so glad I'm your woman.
We can go so much further now. No baggage just
love as I travel down the road of life. Forever till
the end.

No more baggage just my freedom.

No Black Women Allowed

No black women allowed I say,

    Eyes of evil.
    Their mouth poison.
     Their eyes only see what they want.
     Their hearts full of envy and jealousy.

No black woman has ever understood me.
No black woman has been true.
No black woman has tried to see past the envy
and stood by my side.

No black woman has gone the distance; stop short
before the finish line.

So my search for a BLACK woman ends today.
    For my feet are sore.
    My legs are tired.
    To keep reaching out to an empty space.
No more anger- Just no more BLACK WOMEN
HERE!!!!!

<u>No Time</u>

A house full of people and feeling so alone. Waiting in line at an empty store. Kid's everywhere no adult to talk to. Waiting for a turn at the daddy mobile. It goes round and round, getting dizzy trying to catch a ride. I pay the toll but my turn gets skipped.

Crying, screaming and not being heard. I'm not jealous of the children, just want you to know. Just need sometime, sometime alone. Trying to balance a relationship and children is hard to do. Just reminding dad I'm here too. There's a little girl in me wanting to play as well. But too many children and dad can't see me through the trees and the forest.

Once Again

Once again I thought
things were right. Once
again I was wrong, always
assuming we were on the
same page. Just once
I wish that you could
believe in me. Really
listen when I speak. You
select the things you want
to hear. The important
things are not on the top
of your list. The minute
becomes a giant. Please
understand I'm trying real
hard here. But once again
I feel like I'm falling.

Pain

The pain that I've seen is far more
than I wanted to know. The pain
I've felt is more than any woman
should bear. The pain that has me
hunched over. The pain on my sore
fingers. The pain between my legs.
The pain women bear to bring
new life to this world. The pain we
endure every month. We feel pain
every time we say I love you and
the same pain we go through just
to keep you. The pain I feel right
now this very moment in time.
I hurt, I ache, I cry at night. The
pain that my head can bear.

Pain that I just can't get rid of.
What did I do to deserve this
Lord? What did I say? Can you
please end my pain! I want to

live and enjoy life and all it's joy and happiness. I want to feel the sunshine on my face.

So I will embrace my pain and be strong. Be strong. Be strong to live another day.

<u>Questions</u>

Sitting here thinking of you. Wondering what 's going on in your mind and heart. I love you like no other. I care for you. I don't know whether to hate you or love you. It's a toss up, my body longs for your touch. The space between us is growing larger. Our love has filled the void.

What to do with you is the question. I know that I do want you in my life, but on my terms on my time. Being apart has made our relationship stronger. We talk, we communicate and things seem okay. Maybe separate but together is okay. I can't explain it. I'm going with the flow, without question.

Relationships

Not going to run anymore. This feeling has taken over me. The anger that consumes my mind. Trying to be an adult and work things out. Don't scream, don't slam that door, open my eyes and see your pain. Open my ears to hear, what you have to say. I understand your fears and concerns. I just don't think you hear what I'm trying to say.

In a relationship there will be times when the waves get tough. Please understand I'm human and I will make mistakes. But understand that I'm not going anywhere. I'm here till the end. So let's get past this and be friends.

Roots

Roots have no boundarie*s no matter where one lives or where one comes from.*

Like a Willow tree is planted its roots becomes embedded into the soil. They dig deeper into the ground.

The roots determine whether the tree lives or dies. If the tree has strong roots it can survive. This reminds me of what my mother once said: " If you can live in N.Y the hardest place in the world you can live anywhere. " Plant your roots fight to survive – make a stand.

SEE SAW

*Life on the seesaw has its ups and
downs.
On one hand you can be soaring so
high in the sky.
Lying low when life is too hard.*

*Living on the seesaw is very addicting.
You may get sick, but you keep on
playing. Not knowing the game to end.
But on the other hand, there will come a
time. I will go home. Shall I get off of
this ride while the getting is good.*

SELF CONFIDENT

Understanding a woman is an ever changing self. A woman evolves. A woman moves with the shifting planets. A woman can become anyone she wills herself to be. A woman can be molded like clay to what her man wants her to be.

That's why woman gets lost. They lose themselves making it so hard to find it again. When she allows herself to change, it's a pain. She's a lost child or a puppet being pulled by strings. No matter what be true to yourself. Be real. Control your own mind and destiny.

SHORT BUT SWEET

Through your eyes I can see your pure heart.

When our flesh touches it's like the Fourth of July.

When you come inside me. It's like our soul met.

Your touch gives life to my body.

When we made love, it's as if I'm standing in the rain. Rain on me.

Natural, pure, simply safe and sweet.

Sleeplessness

Go to sleep my child. You're not missing any thing.

For life has many surprises for you.

Try to play with the angels that watch over while you sleep.

Just know that mommy will keep you safe.

So close your eyes little baby and embrace the dream. For your family loves you and will keep you from harm while you sleep.

Stepping Out of One's Self

The door opened and he is standing there my heart has stopped. Don't know what to expect. The meeting was planned and I could have changed my mind. Walking through the doorway pushing against his chest. Flashes of the past went thru my mind. "Run girl, run!" My heart screamed. My feet did not responded- my body was lost.

His lips touched mine. No! No! – brain kicked in. "This is wrong for you, he lied to you!" You know what I want and need, he said. Against the cold wall I went, his hand against my chest. His lips just crashed against my neck. Take me. Walking into that room both falling to the bed. I felt my spirit leave me. Floating in my outer body looking down, who are these people. My eyes filled with tears. I knew I should not be there. My soul watched as the minutes went by. As he held my in his arms- him telling me what I needed to hear. Lying there not knowing what to do or say. I let him in.

In that every moment I had control. He did not have a hold on me. I had distance between him and her for the every first time. He was separated from her. When the dance was over my soul returned. The love she once gave to the man so freely without remorse is now gone. Now realizing that she could walk away from this man and be whole again.

<u>Stew</u>

The water is hot the veggies are not.
I'm so hungry is dinner in the pot?
I put my meats, chopped up my
veggies.
Is the stew almost ready?
As the stew heats up and my
appetite is set.
Now I can get my spoon and bowl
and get my taste buds wet.

Tarik

I know behind those eyes there is a
strong child.
Forced to grow up much sooner than
expected. Forced to hide so many
secrets.
You live two lives separate but equal.
The pressure put on you I hope you can
bear the weight. The expectations are too
high to climb.
But be a child not a young man; enjoy any
happiness you can find.
Because when the childhood ends there's
no turning back. Time out- no do over.
Be grateful that we are here for you
whether you need us or not. So walk tall,
be strong and enjoy your life.

The Crazy World

Games are played by kids. Losers always finish last. A race is never over till the last man crosses the finish line. I'm tired of playing games. I'm tired of finishing last. Playing the game by the rules never help me.

Cheaters, liars and thieves finish in the end. The bottom is top and the last play was the first. The fat lady did not sing.

The devil did do it. The puppet master has held the strings too long. Nice guys finish last in this world we call life. The good guy he's lost his wife.

OJ did do it and Michael played with too many boys. Berretta sang like a canary and the judge set them free.

I do not know where this world is going, but I'm running the other way. Trying to stay sane in an insane world. Everything is upside down and the good guys are losing. Stay strong, stay sweet and trying to be sane.

The Guardian

Oh mom I'm not a baby!!! My pre-teen cries. I always need you by my side, say's my nine year old. Can I walk by myself to the store; makes the statement of the twelve year old.
.
As my 9-month cries and I pick him up. My hugs and kisses cheer him up. When I watch all my children sleep, as I place the blanket across their chests. They sleep walk and I guide them back to bed. I want you to know I will always be there.
No matter what.
When you took your first step.

When you feel ill I was there to catch you. Mama will be there. When you are about to make a bad decision I'm whispering in your ear. When you're going to take drugs I'm the hand that guides you to put them away.

When your friends try to make you walk down the wrong path, I'm the crossing guard that makes the detour clear to see.
Look my child I will always be there to guide you. Guardian Angels have nothing on a mother protecting her young.

Fruit of my loins. You may hate my curfews, my stupid two-hour rule. But if something happens to you the news will always ask. Where was the mother? I'm the devil and the angel that sits on your shoulders. I'm the eye of the sparrow, keeping a watchful look out.

So hate me if you want to I'm mama the guardian in the sky.

"The Man Who had it all and did not know it"

He had the money, the house, the kid's and a good woman. He chose to throw it all away. He took my **heart** and he crushed it, with words and attitude.

He truly did not love me or appreciate the sacrifices I made. He had all of me, my heart, my body and my soul. I let my guard down. I gave him the child in me- pure and innocent. I let him touch me in places that no other did. I loved him- unconditionally.

I didn't want his money- just his time. I wanted to be a part of his body and soul. His walls that he put up, keeps me away. His heart shielded and counseled. His time was limited; his space could not be shared. He just **took and took.** Not giving his true love.

Needing peace of mind. I left before my heart died...

The Other Woman

You give her so much of your time. You stand by her side. She pays your bills and gives you money. She wants you all the time.

Your number is always on her list. She gets all of your attention. You see her every day. Even when you're off you still drop by just to say hello. When she calls you, you come running. How can anyone compete? Your married to her, an affair just won't do. She's number one no second place for her. The other women your first true love- your job.

Tierra

You could have been my child in another life. Your eyes, your smile and your funny ways mimic me in many ways. Even though you're not my child, I would walk through fire to help you when you fall.

Tierra my child your other mother is here. To help you, mold you; have no fear. Your real mom has done an excellent job. You have grown up to be so great I could not be more proud. A true treasure untouched by the world.

TWINS

I 'm trying to understand your feelings.
When we are together. We are one mind
and one body. It's like two stars burning
bright and strong together. Two hearts
drumming to the same beat.

*We've experienced so many things
together. Our thoughts, flowing as one.
Just like a mighty river. Sometimes I feel
that we were twins separated at birth.
Living our lives apart, but still feeling
misunderstood, not complete. Brought
together by fate.*

*Finding you was like finding myself
again. You have made me complete.*

Ups and Down

The Ups the downs the total package.
My life has been like a roller coaster.

Ding dong round four. I'm
taking the punches the
                    bruises the lumps. But I'm
still standing.

Punching and fighting back. I will not be
knocked out.
The thing to remember is that I'm a fighter
and this too shall pass.

At the end I will be standing and the battle will
end.

Victory is mine.

Venom

The venom of a snake can kill in one shot.
The snake knows its venom is deadly for
the most part.
It can paralyze and bring grown men
to their feet. Venom so poisonous and
it defeats. Venom comes in so many
strengths. Some stronger than others,
some weak.
If not the snake, a spider all shapes and
sizes. The venom I can handle is the love
bite. It's strong at first and sometimes it
breaks you down.
Venom of love is what I seek. To feel the
rush that completes me.
Complete rush to the heart. Say the
word and I will stand and take the sting.
The strike of Venomous love.

<u>Time</u>

WAKE UP AND BEGIN LIFE. START YOUR ENGINES AND DON'T FALL.

YOUR LIFE CAN BE YOUR WAKE UP CALL.

EVERY MINUTE OF EVERY SECOND IS SO PRECIOUS.

ONCE YOUR LIFE HAS ENDED IT IS OVER. DON'T WASTE THE TIME YOU HAVE, JOIN LIFE. EXPLORE WHAT YOU CAN ACHIEVE.

TAKE A CHANCE. TIME ONLY GOES FORWARD NOT BACK.

IF YOU DON'T ENJOY IT TO THE FULLEST, YOU WILL REGRET IT.

NEVER LIVE THE LIFE OF WONDERING WHAT IF. LIVE YOUR TIME IN THE MOMENT, FOR I AM DONE AND TRIED.

<u>WAR</u>

Knowing whether to stay or go. Walk away or make a stand. Love is a battlefield. So many battles are lost but the war continues, give or take, Lose or win the WAR will go on.

The victor carries the flag and salutes you. My heart is over flowing. The arrows of cupid were short. The blood so sweet was spilled on the floor. The fires of hell could not be put out. War can cut like a knife, slice the soul, hurt, and heal all wounds.

Come to think of it the battle cannot be won or lost just aborted. Let the victory of love cure us all.

What'Z Up?

What'z up is his famous line. A true father in every way. My super hero because he's a good dad. To his children and his family in every way. Tony's a modern dad not afraid to be that good father to his children and wife. He stands by his woman and to me that's a true man. Fatherhood doesn't receive a paycheck. A husband who's true to his heart. If I could pick a dad it would be him. Taller than a single building, able to fight off the bad guys in a snap.

WHAT'Z UP MAN, IT'S LIFE AND HE HAS THE RIGHT STUFF!!!!!

What Happens When The Honeymoon Is Over

When things have changed. When anger
sets in. No more fun and games. The gloves
have come off. Four corners, the fight is on.
Let's get ready to rumble!!!!
What happens when the honeymoon is over?
The things that were once cute get on your
nerves.
The long stares, the awkward silence. Taken
for granted, not feeling appreciated.
When the honeymoon ends, the kisses are
not as often.
The space in the bed gets larger.
The words I love you get lost in translation.
Holding hands is a major feat.
A long slow kiss becomes a peck on the
cheek.
I don't know when it started, but I know
how it may end.
Distance and space.
Two strangers looking into each other's eyes.

What I'm Feeling

What I'm feeling is overwhelmed and stressed out. It chokes me. It takes my breath. I made my list of things to do every week, never enough time and money. What can I do? The struggle of taking care of kids and being a wife.

What I'm feeling is life. Bills, cooking and cleaning a daily routine. It's never clean enough, not enough money to go around.

I'm feeling incomplete, there should be more to me. More that makes me. I'm feeling that I have a higher purpose in life. So I sit and what and I throw the chair out the window. Broken glass on the floor. I can see the light threw the broken pane. I made up my mind I'm going to take charge of my life.

What I'm feeling right now is empowerment and self-reflection. I'm going to make the best of what I have. Four children I have raised very well. Some people have none but I've some. Children are a blessing that I can see now. Maybe my purpose was to spread my seed and raise the flower. Watch it grow to greatness. As for myself proud of me. Proud of who I am and what I'm going to be.

What am I feeling is a new day. I woke up and discovered myself. What I see is a good mother, wife, beautiful person, smart and complete.

What Lies in Her eyes….

When I took my first breath, she was taking one with me. When I took my first step, she was there to catch me.

From my birth till my many falls, she has been there for me. I tried to be the best and not her worst.

She's my world. She's the end to my beginning. My love for her can not be expressed in words. Her loving touch makes me free. To be all that I can be.

No judge, no jury just a mother who loves me.

To my mother Doretha Blazer who's given me so much in just a short lifetime.

when the Man Arrives

Anticipation- the big chill so to speak. I've waited for this moment for a long time. Now it's here, everything has stopped. My heart, my mind, my being is on a plateau. Holding... I'm onto my glory, my moment has arrived. When I saw his face, his eyes, and his smile. I knew. The walk from a distance captured in the space and time. If I didn't know then I know now. I need this man- the piece to the puzzle- the part of my life.